REMAINS

REMAINS

A Collection of Poetry

HEATHER RICHMOND

Mad Zebra Press

Contents

Dedication vii

Heaven 1

Spring 2

Still 3

Mathematician 4

The Ruin of the Before 5

An Archivist in the Castle 7

Illinois I 9

Illinois II 10

Illinois III 12

Illinois IV 14

Illinois V 15

Gradual Versus Catastrophic Change 16

Cornered 18

Marigolds 19

Anniversary	20
Professional	21
Garden	22
Imprinted	23
Evolution	24
Southern	27
Leavings	28
Settling	29
The Way I Swung My Umbrella	30
Flashed and Shimmered	31
Remains	32
True Fall	33
Writing Class	34
Immediate	35
Deepwater	37

For Miranda, who said these look like poems.

!((!
Published by Mad Zebra Press
143 Saint Louis Avenue
Buffalo, New York 14211

Copyright © 2022 by Mad Zebra Press

All rights reserved. No part of this book may be reproduced in any manner whatsoever without written permission except in the case of brief quotations embodied in critical articles and reviews.

First Printing, 2022

ISBN: 978-1-7363124-1-4

Heaven

My daughter asks where we go when we die
I answer Google
I say when we die, we live on in the memories of those who loved us
but then they realize they don't know nearly enough about us
so they frantically type our names into Google
and maybe even the genealogy sites if they're fancy like that.
And they search and they search
hoping some search engine will tell them
why the car made that fateful turn, or how long the cancer was
                                                                growing
before it was detected
and how we felt on the first day of school
and what our relationship was like with our father.
And if they're lucky, they'll find a clue
they can add like a prized possession to their memories of us.
And that's where we live, in those clues in the cloud
when we die.

Spring

Spring is an ominous event
this year:
the grackles and the tennis matches and the
three-legged cat hold dubious charm.
We don't even notice the magnolias
until their petals litter
the street like the neighbor's trash.
Maybe it's those clouds,
the ones that always storm elsewhere,
but even the fat man holding a basketball hoop
in back of a speeding pickup
makes me wish for snow.

Still

Even after it happened, still we sat on soft carpet
in front of the fire while our perfect little girl played around us.
Even after it happened we ate those big Southern meals that your
                                                                father cooks,
his hair grown back after the successful chemotherapy.
Even after it happened, the trees bloomed and the blooms stayed
despite the cold temperatures at night.
Even still.
So my hand still wants to find its way to the place on your belly
where our secret was.
So our girl still plays babies like we were wanted her to.
So those clothes still hang in the closet like ghosts of the future.
Even still.
It's not so bad.

Mathematician

He held a cigarette;
it was the 1950s.
He held it too long, too
close to the page;
contemplating,
note-taking,
sketching equations
in a darkening room.
These years later
sorting his life,
that singed moment clings to my thumb
and I sit, for a moment
contemplating
crackled paper
and faded equations
in a darkening room.

The Ruin of the Before

I stood in the ghost of us
And watched the apocalypse
Unfold slowly
with the summer evening

In the day
Name plates hung above
Empty cubicles like tombstones
Until they didn't

All that remained were
Sad and glassy eyes
Staring down from the sterile castle
At empty parking lots

I pulled the rusted staples from history
And thought of lockjaw
And you and me, aged and desperate
Joints cracking

I would let myself tumble
From hillsides
Into the hum of the honeybees
A thousand stings just for something to feel

As our daughter
splashed in wading pools
rode bicycles, caught fireflies
Lifted her eyes

To the hot air balloons
Drifting above
And waited
for their descent

An Archivist in the Castle

Ladybeetles lie
on the attic floor, coating bare boards,
encircling dead birds
and other bits of things
we prefer not to look at

A few dishes wait
in the drying rack
as if tomorrow someone will lift them
and place them back
in those excellent cherry cupboards
empty now, but for a can of soup
and a knick-knack
or two

Like a prince
pondering a kiss, I caress ancient letters,
examine the cabinets
of her life's work,
and make my plans

to bring her back.

Illinois I

I wasn't prepared for the way
corn husks mingle
with the leaves and scatter
through town after harvest season --
the brittle stalks swept away suddenly,
making way for winter,
exposing the houses on the other side of the field.

I sit, idling, watching graffiti speed by.
Those trains, they don't even slow down
just charge on through to the next town,
their whistles like some frantic piper
the dry husks dancing behind
in the prairie wind.

Illinois II

And yes there is also the wind,
the wind I had not braced for
though I should have known should have
guessed at its howling gale across the prairie
(the prairie that isn't prairie
its flat abundance annihilated in favor of
hogs and corn so many years ago).
That wind it
knocked the wind right out of me
on the coldest days,
threatening frostbite
smacking against my already-numb
body and brain
screaming wake up, wake up
this town isn't hell it's only purgatory
you aren't dead you aren't even dreaming.

So the eyes, tearing and tearing in the
wind (and at home, on the floor, beside pictures of you)
in the solemn cold, feet crunching in grass

stiff with frost in an empty, desperate town
the eyes, blurred with tears, squinted and saw

an impressionistic vision
a fiction I could live with
a quaint, docile land full of good, kind folks
just trying to make it through the week
a high school basketball team
on a winning streak
and that same woman, day after day,
walking her dog outside.

Illinois III

And still the wind blows like a stranger in my house
creeping through the windows
rattling the upstairs walls
startling my brain awake
like the ghost
by my bedside in the last moments of sleep.
Just a dream, but still she stood
short and portentous in her red scarf, heralding
insubstantial sorrows
heralding the wind, which would have come anyway
and yet is stranger in this house
as everything is stranger in this house
since that woman, the ghost my brain invented
came to visit

That woman, in her red scarf, like the babushkas
in the photographs
you sent to me,
standing short and gnarled with branches for brooms.
The women in their red scarves

whispering into the wind, those hesitancies
you whispered over the phone, asking,
"Are you a stranger to me?"

Illinois IV

The sun
may be at once the least
and the most
obvious,
hazy through Amtrak windows
steaming flooded cornfields
always and forever leapfrogging the moon,
competing for the sky
designing paintings for small-town artists,
throwing shafts through clouds and onto fields
dotted with bales of straw.
Silhouetting memories of
your soft face in the early morning.
The sun, often forgotten except to remark
upon, when conversation has stalled,
drenching the uninterrupted landscape
outside my window,
while I sit with blinds drawn,
waiting for your return.

Illinois V

After the summer storms
(and there were many),
birds' nests littered the streets,
lofted from their trees
by tornadic winds.
Bits of eggshell
tiny broken skulls
small, sad mounds of clay
and straw
and string.
These things,
I was not prepared for.

Gradual Versus Catastrophic Change

For me it came
with the seasons'
slow erosion:
water froze inside cracks
and I crumbled
hard rain beat down
etched gullies in me

For you it came
as cataclysmic flood:
the ice dam broke
washed away everything.
The deluge
tore through you
and changed your course.

Now we inspect
the strata

of our new geographies,
one changed in a moment
the other over eons;
both defined
by absence

Cornered

Take a corner of a week between the nine to fives
the corner of a day between cleaning and his return
sit in the corner of a room
look out a corner of the window
at the corner of a peaceful block,
women walking dogs children climbing trees,
wind bending slowly
around the corners of peaceful homes
and make poems no one will see

Marigolds

She hates the marigolds
(ugly stinking of childhood).
There in the dirt
with the Rhodies
and the Mums
(those nicknames like horrid siblings).
They suck too much water
line the house in a strained smile
guarding its secrets.

Anniversary

Today we stood among hemlocks
and listened to snow
melting around us.
You were braver than me:
you crossed the creek
with bold steps.
I watched from the shore
and wiggled my toes
as ice shifted beneath you
but did not break.

Professional

My wardrobe became filled with
button shirts:
solid colors, wrinkle-free poly blends.
Damp and drying
in the spare closet,
they hung with slouched shoulders
and nothing to say,
waiting for my body
to heft them through the day.

Though their two dimensions
would often suffice
as they made their way
from meeting room to cubicle
from driver's seat to sofa.
No one seemed to notice the hangers
protruding from the neck,
bobbing along at a brisk pace.

Garden

Last year's cicada skins
lie empty, still, in the hostas.
Digging, we find a grub
watch it squirm blind in sunlight
bury it again.

The garter snake beneath the tarp
is not poisonous, despite what your mother may say;
though neither do our words fall gently
as we turn clay earth
making plans for the fruits it will yield.

In the drought of summer we will wonder
if we have asked too much of this place.

Imprinted

Did his hands, his lips
leave marks
an imprint of betrayal?
Can you
feel the places on
my skin where
he touched me?
Or does it take time
a slow bruising
so that one day six months from now
you will look at me and know

Evolution

It is the stuff of adolescent poetry.
The small ugly fountain
abandoned outside my door
by previous residents;
the robins sipping fresh
rainwater;
the mother and father doves
perched on the statue's
head, urging their children into flight;
the cats crouched in the window
tense and ready;
you and I behind translucent
curtains, upstairs

And then:
the heat of summer; the fetid,
evaporating water.
The mosquito larvae wriggling
in green, awaiting their days of
sucking blood.

And the sparrow, drowned and drifting
warning the others
to stay away.

And later still,
still that bird
still in the fountain, still
rotting as the water level lowers.
I leave it, watch it
let the body float until it sinks
remember you here
finding that bird
your dismay
you by the water, still
here next to me
the summer morning fresh
(it smelled like Austria, you said)
the bird's death fresh
our end looming
the last moments sacred.

But that bird must have flapped
its wings it must have
kicked those useless
legs it must have
cursed evolution for a moment
and wished itself back in the seas with
gills for lungs
and fins for feet,

much like just for a moment
I wished myself back
in the time before I knew you
when I didn't know what I was
missing when I didn't get this
drowning feeling in your
absence.

Southern

The mockingbirds
are my companions here,
so ordinary, so exotic.
I point to an anole's red warning;
my daughter is transfixed.
She brings me magnolia leaves
like offerings.
The cars drive by slowly, old ladies craning their necks
to see the strangers in the Wilkersons' yard.
No one here looks
like we do.

Leavings

After I leave
you will stand barefoot
in the melted street-snow
left by my boots

After you leave
I will gather your shaved hairs
from the porcelain sink
and lay them on my tongue

Settling

I've forgiven the trees
their lollipop shape,
their barren months

I've forgiven the sky
its clear blue days
its hard rain

I've forgiven the horizon
for its lack of snowy peaks
to hold the sky in place

and I've forgiven you
for not being another,
whose memory fades

to myth

The Way I Swung My Umbrella

I forgot to tell you how much I love
the way the rain drips
from my gutters
and splashes in the puddles
on my driveway

and I forgot to mention
the way I swung my umbrella
on the way home
the night after we met

Flashed and Shimmered

I grinned at you in the sun,
squinting to see if you would catch
my meaning.

Your bicycle flashed and shimmered
as you buckled your helmet.
You smiled back
(that same smile that makes everyone fall in love with you)

and rode away.

Remains

I had forgotten:
after the snow melts, the leaves remain
moldering against fresh petals.
How I loved
those exposed veins;
delicate lace of my childhood.
I sat among the maples, staring at the sun
through the skeletons of seasons past.

Now I sit inside, shuffling yellowed papers
piecing together remains
of lives long since lived.
Smoothing translucent onion
skin, I hold a crisp page
to the sunlight
look for the lines where
life once flowed.

True Fall

The drought brought a false
autumn --
dead leaves sacrificed
by desperate trees.

Then rain revealed
what had survived --
bulbs confused into sprouting
bare patches of clay soil.

When trees began to yellow
and leaves fell in their own time,
we knew what we had lost.

Writing Class

He asked us, our twenty-year-old selves, "Why are you here?"
I came first and they all watched my lips, but
how do you disclose to a room full of strangers
the thing that glows inside
and keeps you from breaking?
Holding close that secret I said instead
"Because I like to write"
He said, "WRONG"
and corrected my answer with his own.
I watched in horror,
as one by one, each of them
repeated
the lesson.

Immediate

There is nothing immediate
about these moments.

Time drips through the leaky faucet,
seeps through the windowpanes,
surrounds the house in the myth
that motion cures grief
that newness equals change.

Neither are true;
I still forget to water my plants
even as those pothos and umbrella trees of the past
become mulch.
I still doze on the sofa,
book open on my chest

And while some nights I expect
you to wander in from another room
and sit down next to me,
most nights I realize

I hadn't expected that in years.

Deepwater

In Deepwater
we lived in the old schoolhouse,
sat in the upstairs apartment,
watched newscasters report record heat.
The air conditioner
ground through our thoughts and words,
turned them to dust.
Grandchildren played listlessly near
Geri's filthy sofa, and
Iggy the Iguana
perched on the lamp like a frozen thing.
The heat made us monsters;
we'd worn out our welcome and Wilmer
accused us of stealing the nail gun.
The attic was too hot so we slept
in chairs, all of us,
in the living room.
No one would touch Geri's filthy sofa
except Geri.

I heard of the fire from afar,
the fire that burned the old schoolhouse down.
Geri moved from that sofa for the first time in years.
She grabbed the kitten and ran;
Iggy the Iguana burned.
The flames tore through tattered possessions,
put the filthy sofa to rest.
The new apartment had central air.

www.ingramcontent.com/pod-product-compliance
Lightning Source LLC
Chambersburg PA
CBHW020915080526
44589CB00011B/610